HEALTH HELPERS

DENTIST

URSULA PANG

PowerKiDS press

Published in 2026 by The Rosen Publishing Group, Inc.
2544 Clinton Street, Buffalo, NY 14224

First Edition

Editor: Greg Roza
Book Design: Rachel Rising

Photo Credits: Cover, p. 1 Prostock-studio/Shutterstock.com; pp. 4, 6, 8, 10, 12, 14, 16, 18, 20 TechSolution/Shutterstock.com; p. 5 Harbucks/Shutterstock.com; p. 7 SofikoS/Shutterstock.com; p. 9 Dmytro Zinkevych/Shutterstock.com; p. 11 Pop Paul-Catalin/Shutterstock.com; p. 13 Lighthunter/Shutterstock.com; p. 15 Aaaarianne/Shutterstock.com; p. 17 daniiD/Shutterstock.com; p. 19 Pixel-Shot/Shutterstock.com; p. 21 michaeljung/Shutterstock.com.

Names: Pang, Ursula.
Title: Dentist / Ursula Pang.
Description: Buffalo, New York : PowerKids Press, 2026. | Series: Health helpers | Includes glossary and index.
Identifiers: ISBN 9781499456462 (pbk.) | ISBN 9781499456479 (library bound) | ISBN 9781499456486 (ebook)
Subjects: LCSH: Dentists–Juvenile literature. | Dentistry–Juvenile literature. | Dental care–Juvenile literature.
Classification: LCC RK63.P36 2026 | DDC 617.6–dc23

Manufactured in China

CPSIA Compliance Information: Batch #QWPK26. For Further Information contact Rosen Publishing at 1-800-237-9932.

CONTENTS

Meet the Dentist!

Everyone should go to the dentist twice a year. Most often this is for a check-up and a cleaning. Dentists are health helpers who teach us how to care for our teeth. Sometimes people have tooth pain. The dentist will find out why.

Time for a Check-Up

Once you sit down in the dentist's chair, the dentist will use a small mirror and a dental pick to look at your teeth and gums. They will ask you questions such as: Do you feel any pain? Have you been brushing and flossing every day?

Cleaning Teeth

Next, the dentist will use dental tools to clean your teeth. The tools include several kinds of picks. They use the picks to **scrape** teeth clean. Then, they will floss between your teeth. Last, they will use another tool to **polish** your teeth.

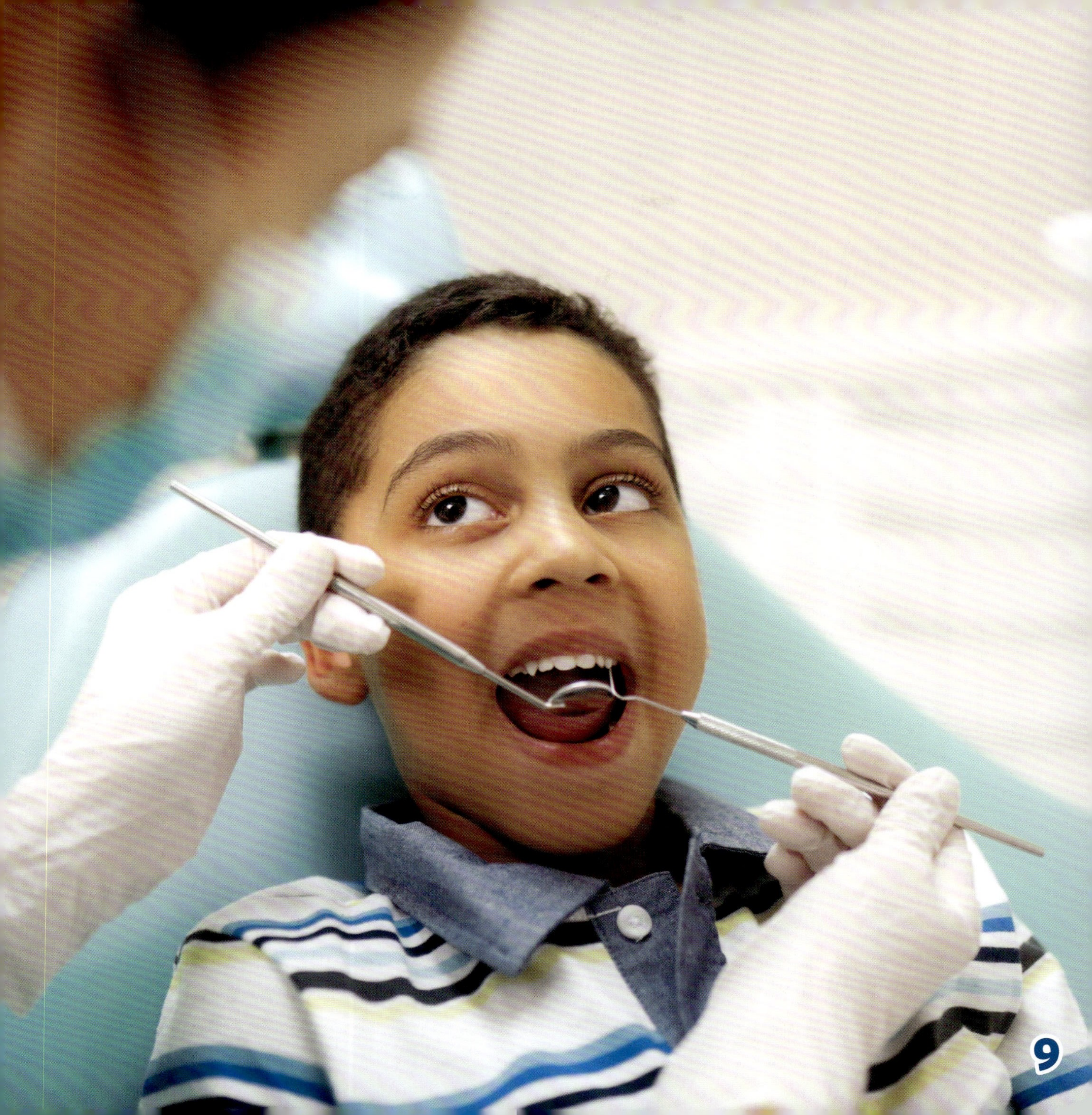

Plaque and Cavities

Why does the dentist scrape your teeth? To remove plaque! Plaque is a hard matter that forms on and between teeth. If left alone, plaque can lead to tooth **decay** and **cavities**. You can fight plaque build-up by brushing, flossing, and going to the dentist.

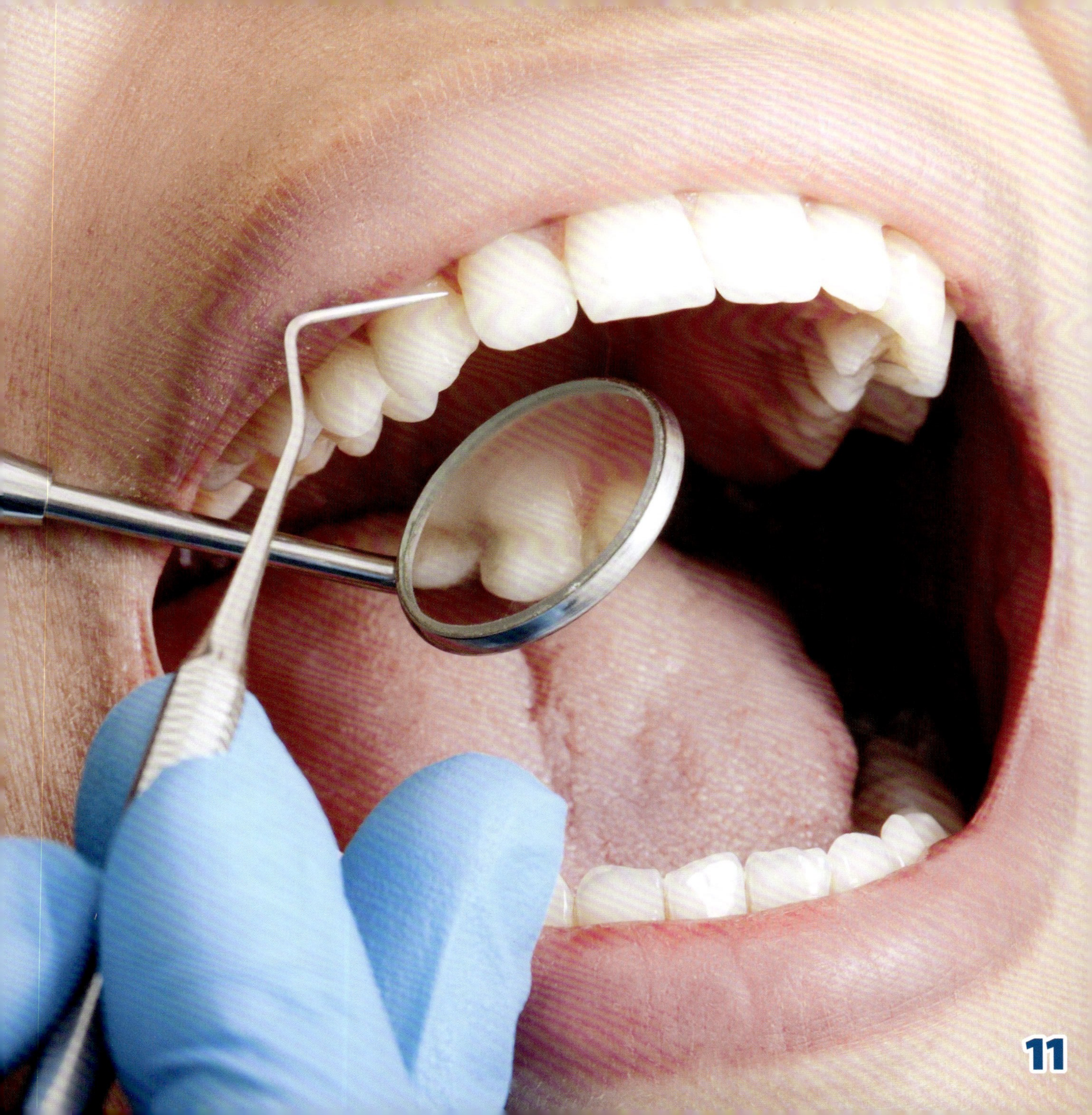

If you have a cavity, the dentist will remove the tooth decay. They use a tiny drill to do this. They will give you a shot so you don't feel anything. After removing the decay, the hole is filled with dental material that hardens. No more cavity!

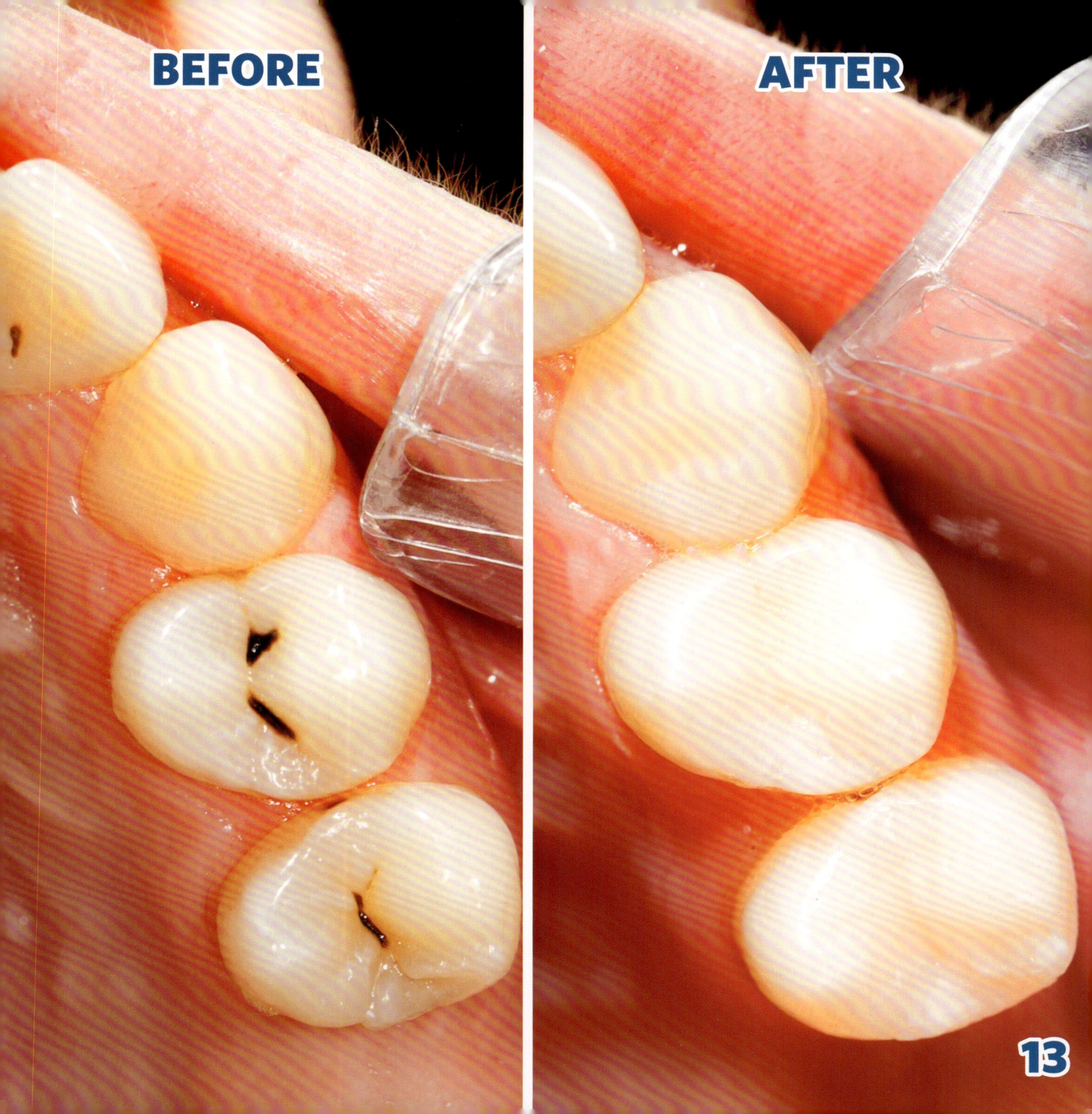
BEFORE
AFTER

What Is Gingivitis?

Plaque can affect your gums. This can cause gingivitis, which is an early form of gum **disease**. The gums become red, **swollen**, and painful. They may also bleed when flossing or eating. If you have gingivitis, the dentist may need to scrape your teeth below the gum line.

X-rays

X-rays are medical images that show the inside of the body. Dental X-rays show the dentist where you need to brush better. They will see if cavities are growing. X-rays also show wisdom teeth. Most people have their wisdom teeth removed because they often cause pain.

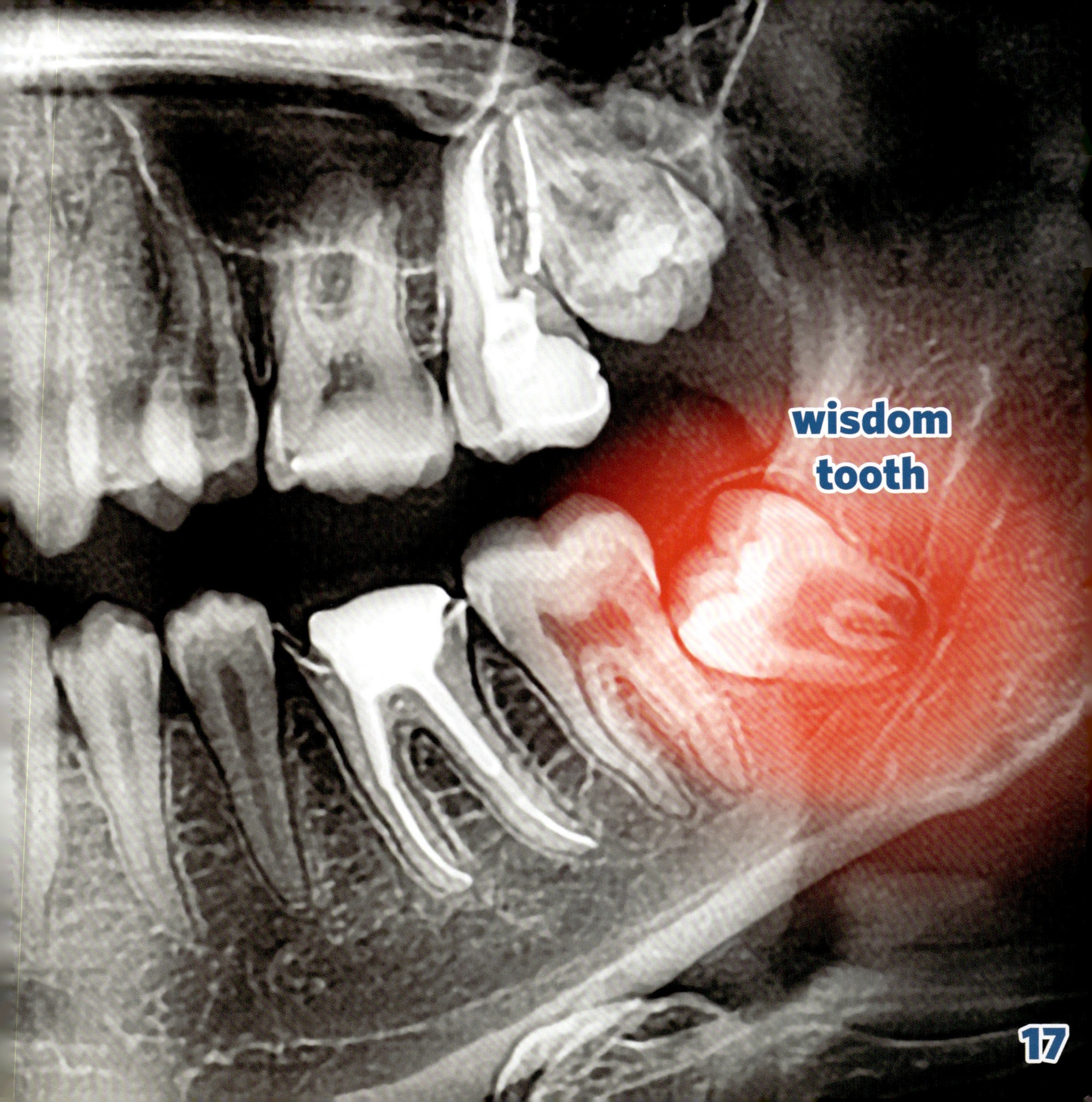
wisdom
tooth

What Do Orthodontists Do?

Sometimes teeth grow unevenly. They may not line up right. This can cause mouth pain. The dentist will send you to an orthodontist. Orthodontists are dentists who specialize in braces. Braces are dental tools that straighten teeth. Some are metal. Others are plastic.

Time to Smile!

Dentists and orthodontists are health helpers who care about the health of your teeth! They are trained to give special care with the least pain possible. They also teach people how to avoid getting cavities in the first place—brushing and flossing!

GLOSSARY

cavity: An open space, and an area of tooth decay on a tooth.

decay: Rot.

disease: A sickness.

polish: To rub something to make it smooth and shiny.

scrape: To remove something using a tool with a sharp edge.

swollen: To become larger or puffed up.

FOR MORE INFORMATION

BOOKS

Hanger, Sarah. *My First Visit to the Orthodontist.* West Palm Beach, FL: Ballast Books, 2024.

Kukla, Lauren. *I'm a Dentist.* Rochester, MN: Mayo Clinic Press, 2025.

WEBSITES

Going to the Dentist
kidshealth.org/en/kids/go-dentist.html
Read more about what goes on in a dentist's office.

What's an Orthodontist?
kidshealth.org/en/kids/orthodontist.html?ref=search
This webpage offers more information about orthodontists and braces.

INDEX